SHELLY SHAZAM!

ABBY SEGAL

Dedicated to my grandma.

A magician performs at Shelly's school today.

She does all sorts of magic tricks that amaze Shelly and her classmates.

After the show, Shelly goes up to the magician and asks if she can learn a magic trick.

The magician shares the secret to making a coin disappear from her hand.

When Shelly says the magic words and opens her hand, she is amazed that she can do magic too!

Shelly's family is throwing her Grandma a big birthday party tonight.

How cool would it be if she performs the disappearing coin trick for her Grandma and the guests?

But first, she needs to practice.

At the playground, she wants to show her friends the coin trick, but she made the coin disappear!

Shelly scratches her head,
Squints her eyes,
And looks all around

Can she find something as small as a coin to use instead?

SHELLY SHAZAM!
She can do the trick with...

A PEBBLE!

Then in the car, Shelly wants to show her Dad the pebble trick, but she made the pebble disappear!

Shelly scratches her head,
Squints her eyes,
And looks all around

Can she find something as small as a pebble to use instead?

SHELLY SHAZAM!
She can do the trick with...

A BOTTLE CAP!

At the post office, Shelly wants to show the postal worker the bottle cap trick, but she made the cap disappear!

Shelly scratches her head,
Squints her eyes,
And looks all around

Can she find something as small as a bottle cap to use instead?

SHELLY SHAZAM!
She can do the trick with...

A STAMP!

KEVIN

Then in the center of town, there is a checkers tournament going on. Shelly wants to show the players the stamp trick, but she made the stamp disappear!
BAKERY
POST OFFICE
FLOWER SHOP
OPEN

Shelly scratches her head,
Squints her eyes,
And looks all around

Can she find something as small as a stamp to use instead?

FFICE
FLOWER SHOP
OPEN
SHELLY SHAZAM!
She can do the trick with...

A CHECKERS PIECE!

At the pizza joint, Shelly wants to show the pizza man the checker piece trick, but she made the piece disappear!

Shelly scratches her head,
Squints her eyes,
And looks all around

Can she find something as small as a checkers piece to use instead?

SHELLY SHAZAM!
She can do the trick with...

A PEPPERONI SLICE!

Then at home, it's time to get ready for the party.

BIRTHDAY QUEEN
Everyone is having a great time at
Grandma's birthday party.

After Grandma opens her presents, all of her
guests surround Shelly so she can perform the
trick the magician taught her.

She just needs a small object to perform the trick with.

Shelly scratches her head,
Squints her eyes,
And looks all around

MAGIC LENS

SHELLY
SHA-

Wait a second! She can't find anything to make disappear!

What is she going to do?!

Shelly starts to panic but then...

SHELLY
SHAZAM!

She can make everything she made disappear...

REAPPEAR!!

After Grandma's party, Shelly puts all of the small magical items in her secret box. What will she make disappear and reappear next?

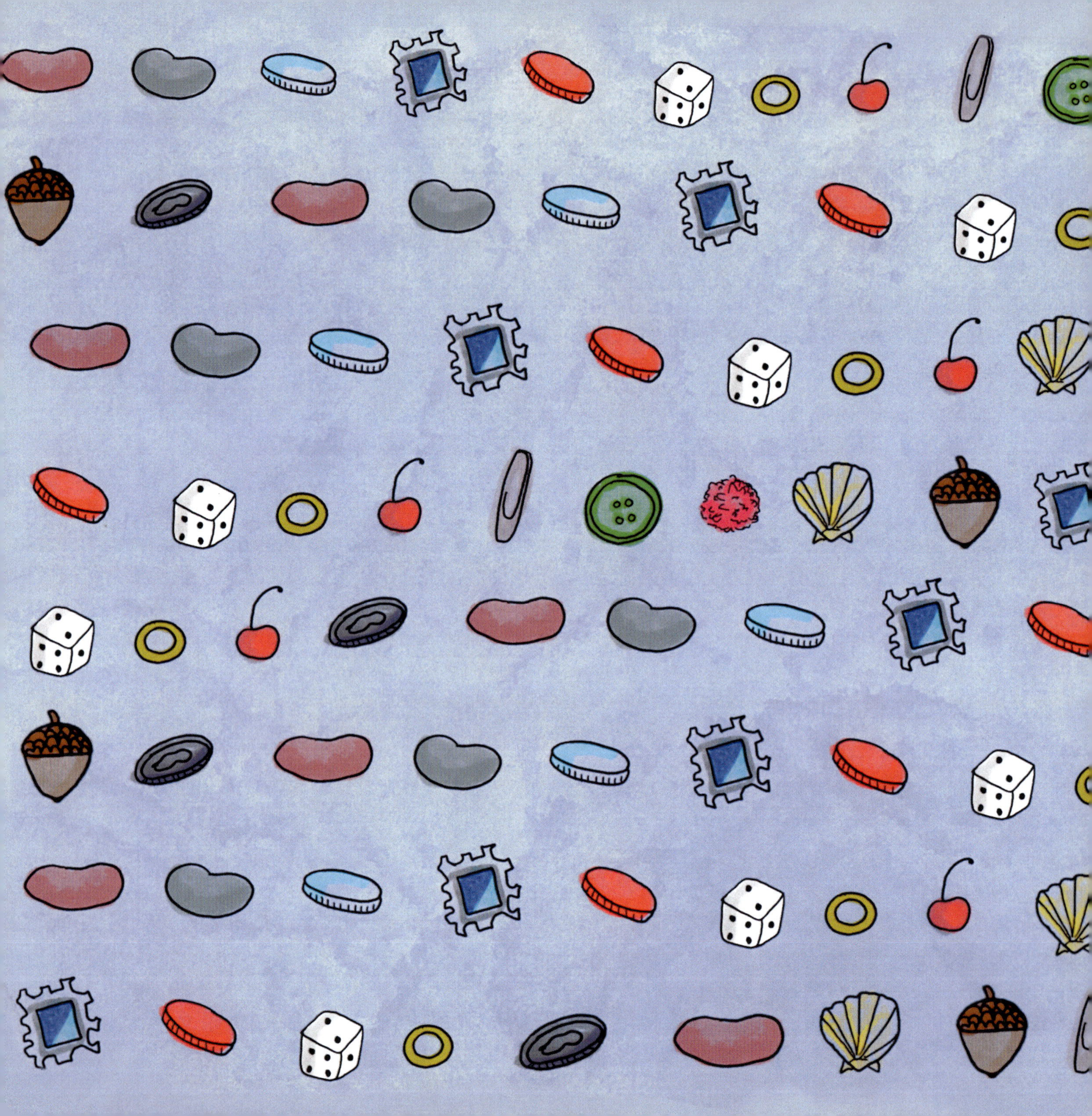

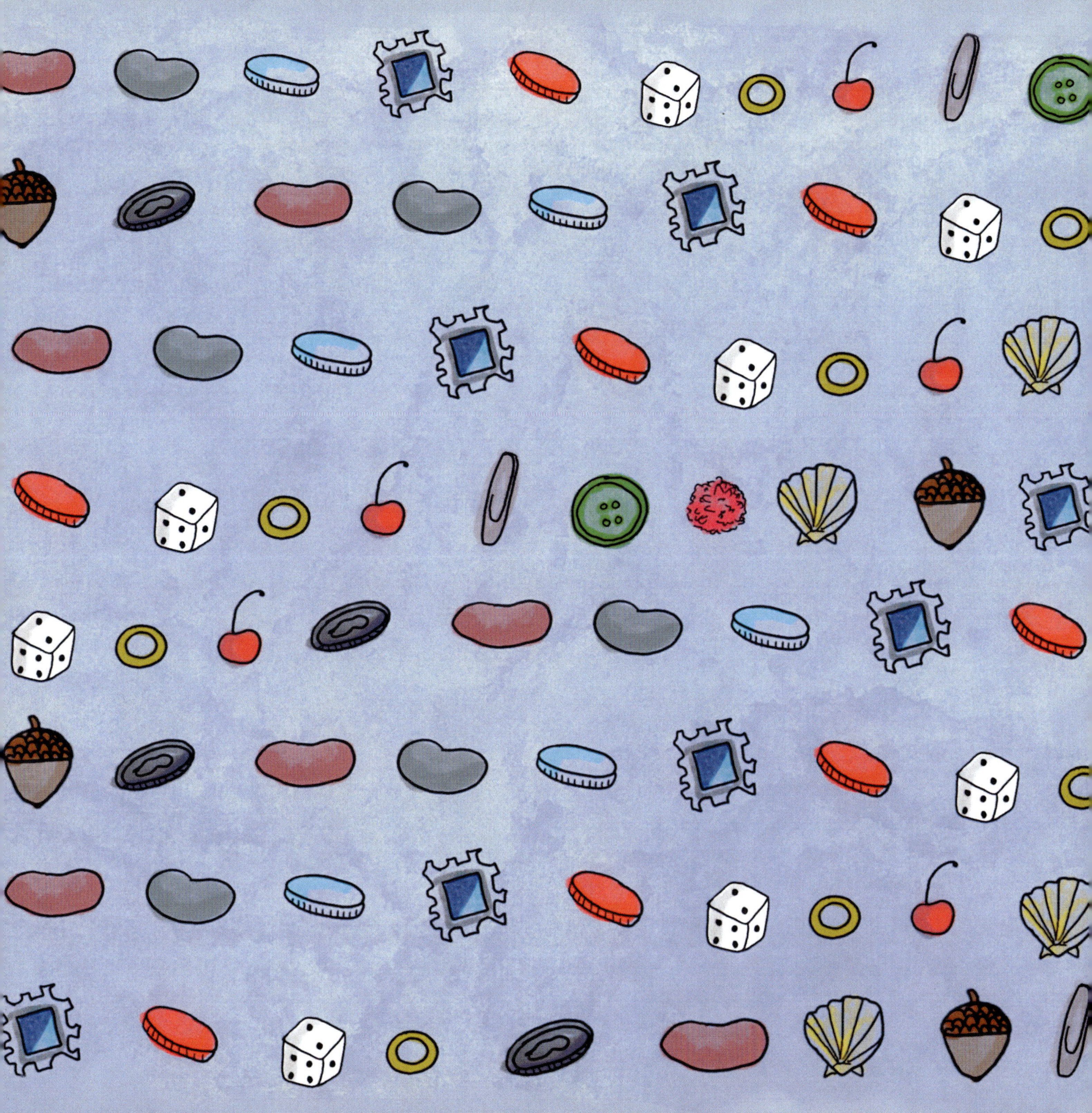

ABOUT THE AUTHOR

Abby Segal is 22 years old from Chelmsford, Massachusetts. She recently graduated from Bates College with a B.A. in Psychology. Along with her passion for writing and illustrating, Abby works as a professional magician for private events, and is a regular performer at the Chicago Magic Lounge. Abby has been a magician since she was 11 years old and has been drawing and writing stories since she was Shelly's age. Abby sees the world like Shelly-with open eyes, ready to create and imagine at any moment. Abby wants to invite her young readers to explore their own imagination and creativity by interacting with the world around them!

Made in United States
North Haven, CT
22 June 2023